PTERODACTYLS

A TRUE BOOK

by
Elaine Landau

Children's Press®
A Division of Grolier Publishing

New York London Hong Kong Sydney
Danbury, Connecticut

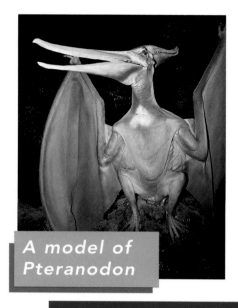

A model of
Pteranodon

Reading Consultant
Linda Cornwell
*Coordinator Of School Quality
And Professional Improvement
Indiana State Teachers Association*

Science Consultant
James O. Farlow
*Indiana University-
Prudue University, Fort Wayne
Department of Geosciences*

*Dedication:
For Michael, who is more fun
than any prehistoric reptile*

Visit Children's Press® on the Internet at:
http://publishing.grolier.com

Library of Congress Cataloging-in-Publication Data

Landau, Elaine.
    Pterodactyls / by Elaine Landau.
        p.   cm. — (A true book)
        Includes bibliographical references (p. -) and index.
        Summary: Describes the characteristics and behavior of the extinct
flying reptiles that lived on the Earth during the Mesozoic era.
        ISBN 0-516-20447-5 (lib.bdg.)   0-516-26500-8 (pbk.)
        1. Pterodactyls—Juvenile literature. [1. Pterodactyls.
    2. Prehistoric animals.] I. Title. II. Series.
    QE862.P7L36   1999
    567.918—dc21   98-8280
                                                                        CIP
                                                                        AC

Contents

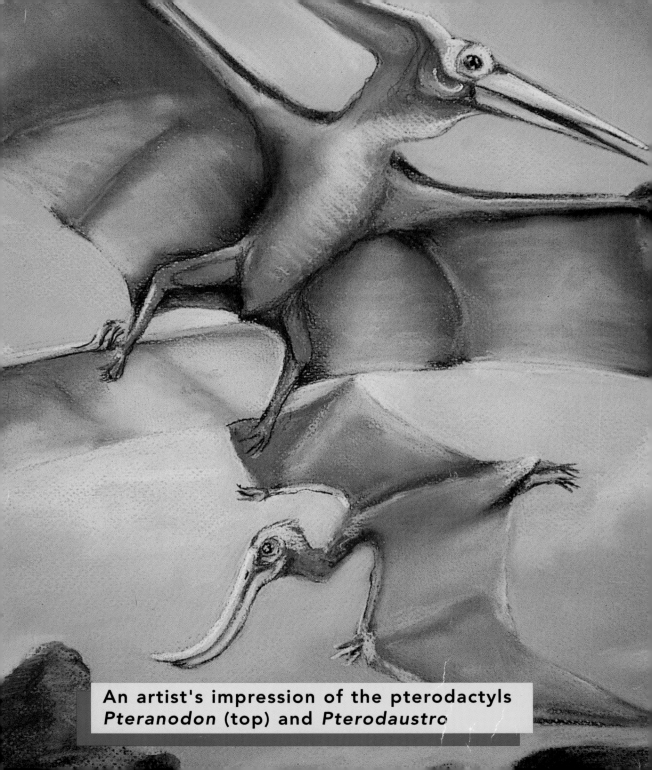

An artist's impression of the pterodactyls *Pteranodon* (top) and *Pterodaustro*

What's That in the Air?

It's a bird . . .

It's a plane . . .

It's Superman . . .

No, it's a pterodactyl! That's what you might have said looking up at the sky many millions of years ago. Of course, there were no people on Earth then. Instead, the

world was filled with many different kinds of ancient reptiles.
Flying reptiles, called
pterosaurs, glided through the
air. Certain types of pterosaurs
were called pterodactyls.
Dinosaurs—reptiles that lived

Some creatures that lived on Earth
about 165 million years ago

on land—roamed the Earth below. Huge marine reptiles that looked like sea serpents swam in the waters. All this took place during the Mesozoic era, the time period from about 245 million to about 65 million years ago.

There were two types of pterosaurs. The earliest pterosaurs were called rhamphorhynchoids. They appeared late in the Triassic period (the first part of the Mesozoic era).

A fossil of *Rhamphorhynchus*, an early pterosaur

These flying reptiles had short legs and long, bony tails. Rhamphorhyncoids became extinct at the end of the Jurassic period (the middle part of the Mesozoic era).

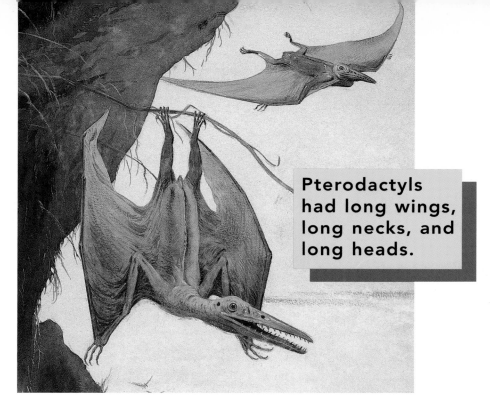

Pterodactyls had long wings, long necks, and long heads.

Pterodactyloids, also called pterodactyls, first appeared during the Late Jurassic period. There were different kinds of pterodactyls, but they all had long wings, long necks, and long heads. In some cases,

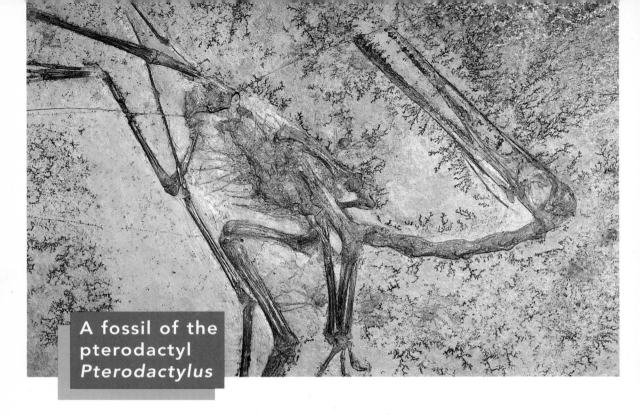

A fossil of the pterodactyl *Pterodactylus*

their heads were as long as or even longer than the rest of their bodies. Pterodactyls also had short tails.

How do we know what pterodactyls looked like? Paleontologists, scientists who study prehistoric life, have pieced together information about pterodactyls and other prehistoric animals by looking at fossils. Fossils are animal or plant remains—such as bones, tissues, or skin—that have been buried in the Earth's crust for thousands or millions of years.

Some pterodactyls were quite big. But even the largest ones had lightweight bones that were hollow. This was important for flight.

Wings were attached to the long fourth fingers of pterodactyls.

One of the most interesting features of pterodactyls was their fingers. Pterodactyls had three short fingers with claws. Their fourth fingers, however, were extremely long. Their wings were attached to these.

Although pterodactyls flew, they were not related to birds. Birds evolved independently of any winged reptile. Unlike birds, flying reptiles did not have feathers.

Early pterodactyls were different from the types that came along later. The early pterodactyls had teeth. These, however, eventually died out and were replaced by toothless pterodactyls with long beaks.

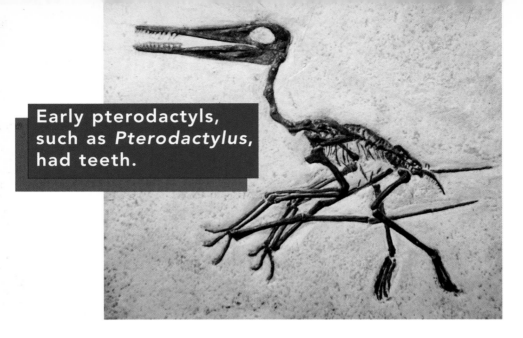

Early pterodactyls, such as *Pterodactylus*, had teeth.

Some of the earlier pterodactyls had also been quite small. Several were only the size of a robin or sparrow. Near the end of the Cretaceous period (the last part of the Mesozoic era), very large pterodactyls became common. One type was as big as a small plane!

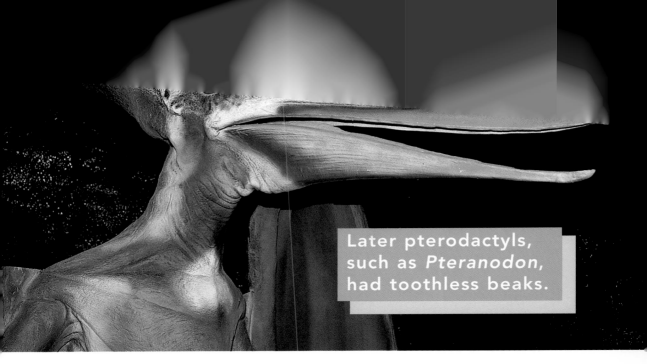

Later pterodactyls, such as *Pteranodon*, had toothless beaks.

It may be hard to think of a flying creature that was not an insect or a bird. But this interesting group of flying prehistoric reptiles really existed. Some of the better-known pterodactyls are described in the following pages.

Pterodactylus

Pterodactylus

Pterodactylus existed toward the end of the Jurassic period. It was not a very big pterodactyl. It had a wingspread of up to about 2.5 feet (0.7 m). It had long, narrow jaws and fairly sharp teeth. Scientists think this small winged reptile was a good flyer. It probably fed on insects or small fish.

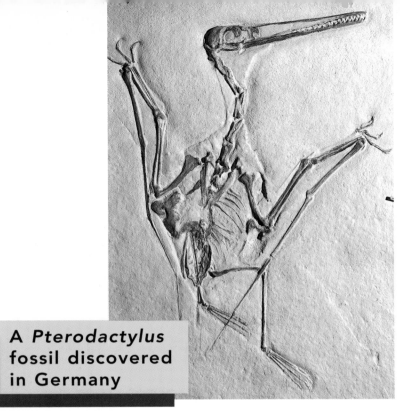

A *Pterodactylus* fossil discovered in Germany

Pterodactylus fossils have been found in Africa and Europe. In fact, the first pterosaur fossil ever described was a *Pterodactylus* fossil. It was discovered in Germany in the 1700s.

An inaccurate 19th-century drawing of pterosaurs

Mistaken Identity

The first pterosaur fossils were discovered in the 1700s. But at the time, scientists didn't realize what they'd found. They mistakenly thought the fossils belonged to some type of sea creature or bat. Only later did researchers learn that they'd actually been studying the remains of a prehistoric flyer.

Pterodaustro

*P*terodaustro

This flying reptile lived in South America during the Early Cretaceous period. It was larger than *Pterodactylus*. Its wing-spread was about 4 feet (1.2 m). The non-wing fingers of *Pterodaustro* were among the smallest of all pterosaurs. *Pterodaustro's* feet were among the largest of pterosaurs.

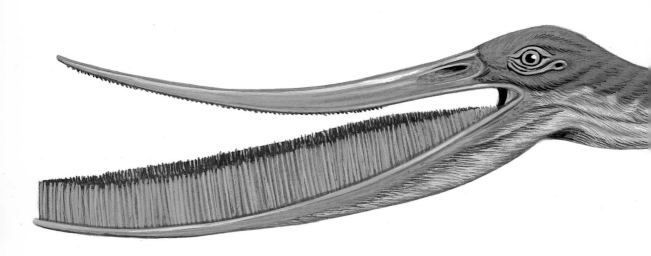

What made *Pterodaustro* interesting were its jaws. It had long, thin jaws that curved upwards. Its lower jaw was packed with hundreds of long, thin teeth—up to five hundred teeth on each side! The jaw of *Pterodaustro* has been compared to a fine-toothed comb. The upper jaw had short teeth that combed through the lower teeth.

Scientists think that *Pterodaustro* fed on fish and small water animals. It probably flew right over the sea with its mouth open. As the water flowed through its jaws, its lower teeth trapped the prey.

Pteranodon

Pteranodon

With a wingspread of 23 feet (7 m), *Pteranodon* was among the larger pterodactyls. This toothless winged reptile had an extremely long neck and beak. It also had very large wings that allowed it to glide easily through the air.

Pteranodon had a bony crest at the back of its head.

Scientists think *Pteranodon* may have taken its prey from the ocean. It could have plucked fish from the water with its long beak and swallowed them whole. Like today's pelicans, it had a roomy skin pouch beneath its lower jaw for storing fish.

Pteranodon had a large bone crest growing out of the back of its head. Scientists aren't sure how the crest was used. It may have helped *Pteranodon* keep its balance in flight. Or perhaps it steadied this fish eater when it reached forward to snatch a fish with its long beak.

Pteranodon lived late in the Cretaceous period. Its fossils have been found in England and North America.

Quetzalcoatlus

Quetzalcoatlus

Quetzalcoatlus was the largest flying animal that has ever lived. It appeared in the area that is now Texas about 68 million years ago, near the end of the Cretaceous period.

This prehistoric reptile's body was about 20 feet (6 m) long. It had a wingspread of

A museum model of *Quetzalcoatlus*

about 40 feet (12 m)! Even its beak was about 6 feet (1.8 m) long. That's the height of a fairly tall human male!

The whooping crane is the largest bird in the United States today. *Quetzalcoatlus* was five times the size of a whooping crane. In flight, *Quetzalcoatlus* may have looked like a living aircraft.

Some scientists think *Quetzalcoatlus* fed on animal remains. Perhaps it spied decaying dinosaur bodies or other dead animals from the air. After swooping down, *Quetzalcoatlus* would have picked through the remains with its beak. Once it had its fill, it would take off again.

A life-sized model of *Pteranodon*

A Prehistoric Mystery

Over the years, scientists have learned a lot about pterodactyls. But there's still much more to know. Some important questions about pterodactyls were discussed at a recent meeting of the Society of Vertebrate Paleontology.

At that time, scientists agreed that we need to know more about the way these winged reptiles flew. How did they take off? Did they run along the ground, or did they drop from a cliff or high tree branch? Did they glide, or flap their wings to fly?

Paleontologists have different opinions on this. Some insist that pterodactyls were too large and clumsy to reach the sky directly from the

This life-sized model of *Pteranodon* was designed to imitate the way the actual reptile may have flown.

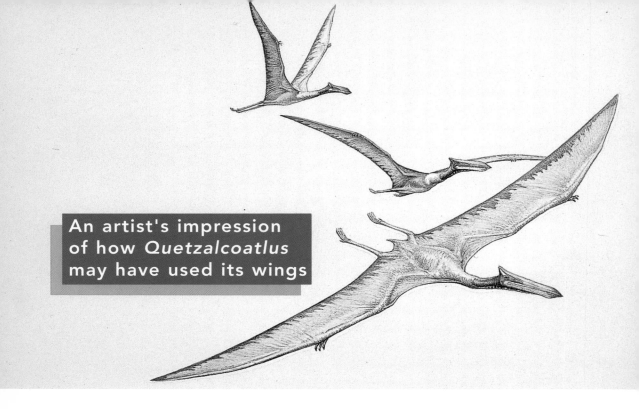

An artist's impression of how *Quetzalcoatlus* may have used its wings

ground. But others point to the numerous hardened pterodactyl footprints found on land. They argue that these prove that winged reptiles had to have taken off from the ground. No one can be certain.

There are other important questions about these prehistoric flyers as well. When not in flight, did these reptiles walk on two feet, as birds do? Or did they crawl about on all fours, like bats? Once again, the experts disagree. Judging from some footprints, a number of scientists insist that pterodactyls crawled. But others have pointed to different footprints to argue the opposite.

Scientists also want to know more about the daily lives of pterodactyls. Did these flying reptiles usually remain alone? Or did pterodactyls form colonies? As you might expect, the experts have varied views on this too.

Future research may provide some more solid answers. Recently, a number of pterodactyl fossils were discovered in Chile. The Chilean find suggests that pterodactyls may have lived in groups.

Extinction

Many people think ptero-
dactyls and dinosaurs became
extinct all at the same time.
But that is only partly correct.

Various kinds of ancient reptiles lived—and then became
extinct—at different times during the Mesozoic era. No one
knows why certain types died

out when they did. Then, about 65 million years ago, all the remaining pterodactyls and dinosaurs, as well as most other forms of life on Earth, died out.

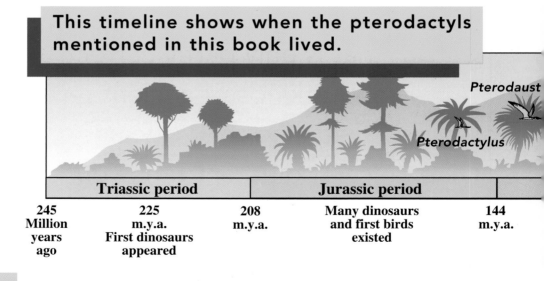

This timeline shows when the pterodactyls mentioned in this book lived.

Pterodaust

Pterodactylus

	Triassic period		Jurassic period	
245 Million years ago	225 m.y.a. First dinosaurs appeared	208 m.y.a.	Many dinosaurs and first birds existed	144 m.y.a.

Scientists have several theories about why this happened. One theory is that a comet or asteroid crashed into Earth. The dust thrown up from the huge crater caused by this

Quetzalcoatlus

Pteranodon

| Cretaceous period | Tertiary period | |

65
m.y.a.
**Last dinosaurs
became extinct**

1.6
m.y.a.
**First humans
appeared**

Fossils like this are all we have left of pterodactyls.

crash would have floated up into the atmosphere. It would have formed thick, dark clouds blocking out the Sun.

Without the Sun's warmth, Earth's climate would have turned quite cold. Dinosaurs and other forms of life would not have been able to survive this weather change.

We may never know as much as we'd like to about pterodactyls. That's because they died out completely and have no relatives in the modern animal world. This makes it more difficult for scientists to study their behavior. In some ways, these prehistoric flyers may always remain a mystery of the past.

To Find Out More

Here are some additional resources to help you learn more about pterodactyls:

 **Books**

Aliki. **Fossils Tell of Long Ago.** Crowell, 1990.

Gamlin, Linda. **Evolution.** Dorling Kindersley, 1993.

Henderson, Douglas. **Dinosaur Tree.** Bradbury Press, 1994.

Lindsay, William. **Prehistoric Life.** Knopf, 1994.

McCarthy, Colin. **Reptile.** Knopf, 1991.

Rand McNally Picture Atlas of Prehistoric Life. Rand McNally, 1992.

Taylor, Paul D. **Fossil.** Knopf, 1990.

The Visual Dictionary of Prehistoric Life. Knopf, 1994.

Whitfield, Philip J. **Macmillan's Children's Guide to Dinosaurs and Other Prehistoric Animals.** Macmillan, 1992.

Organizations and Online Sites

The American Museum of Natural History
Central Park West at
79th Street
New York, NY 10024
http://www.amnh.org

One of the world's largest natural-history museums, it has exceptional collections on dinosaurs and other prehistoric animals.

Dinorama
http://www. nationalgeographic.com/ dinorama/frame.html

A *National Geographic* site with information about dinosaurs and current methods of learning about them. Includes timelines, animations, and fun facts.

National Museum of Natural History,
Smithsonian Institution
10th Street and
Constitution Ave. NW
Washington, D.C.
http://www.mnh.si.edu/ nmnhweb.html

In the museum's Dinosaur Hall, you can see real fossils of dinosaurs and pterodactyls.

ZoomDinosaurs
http://www. ZoomDinosaurs.com/

Contains everything you might want to know about dinosaurs and other ancient reptiles. It has separate pages on pterosaurs, pterodactyls, *Pteranodon*, and *Quetzalcoatlus*, and each includes facts, myths, activities, a geologic time chart, print-outs, and links.

Important Words

asteroid rocky, planetlike object orbiting in space

comet frozen ball of water, gases, and dust from the farthest reaches of our solar system

evolved changed or came to be over a long period of time

extinct no longer in existence

independently separate from

prehistoric existing before humans began recording history

prey animal hunted by another animal for food

remains bones or tissue left behind after an animal or plant dies

vertebrate having a backbone

wingspread in a winged animal, the distance from the tip of one wing to the tip of the other wing

Index

Meet the Author

Elaine Landau has a Bachelor of Arts degree in English and Journalism from New York University and a Master's degree in Library and Information Science from Pratt Institute. She has worked as a newspaper reporter, children's book editor, and youth-services librarian, but especially enjoys writing for young people.

Ms. Landau has written more than a hundred nonfiction books on various topics. She lives in Miami, Florida, with her husband, Norman, and son, Michael.

Photographs ©: AKG London: 19, 42; Ben Klaffke: 4, 26 right; Bridgeman Art Library International Ltd., London/New York: 6 (Natural History Museum, London, UK); Jay Mallin: 30; Museum of the Rockies: 12 (Bruce Selyem); Natural History Museum, London: 9 (Painting by Neave Parker), 36 (J. Sibbick); Photo Researchers: 26 left, 32, 35 (Martin Dohrn), 8 (California Academy of Sciences/Tom McHugh); Tom Stack & Associates: 2, 15 (Brian Parker); Visuals Unlimited: 14 (J. Copley), 10, 18 (Ken Lucas). Illustrations by Greg Harris